AI Gadget

The Rabbit R1 App Handler

Matthew H. Larsen

Copyright

About the Author

In the fields of science and artificial intelligence, Matthew H. Larsen is a well-known figure. Larsen has a strong academic background in computer science and years of experience working in the tech business. He has made a name for himself as a forward-thinker and an innovator. He started his journey with a degree in Computer Science and then moved on to get a Master's in Artificial Intelligence, where he learned more about machine learning, robots, and the ethics of AI.

Larsen's work life is marked by his time at several top tech companies, where he was a key figure in creating AI-powered technologies. Not only is he good at developing technology, but he's also good at picturing how AI could be used in everyday life. Because he has so many skills, companies that want to use AI in their work often hire him as a consultant.

Matthew is a professional, but he also loves writing and speaking in public. He often writes for tech blogs and magazines, talking about the newest developments in AI and how they affect society. He put on workshops and lectures to demystify AI and make it easier for a wider audience to understand because he loved teaching others.

The author of "AI Gadget: The Rabbit R1 App Handler," Larsen distills his vast knowledge and experience into this comprehensive guide, making it a must-read for anyone interested in the practical applications of AI. His writing style is helpful and interesting, so it's good for both tech experts and people who are just starting out.

Matthew H. Larsen is not just an author but a visionary who tries to bridge the gap between complicated AI technologies and everyday users. His book shows his commitment to this cause, giving valuable insights into the world of AI-powered gadgets and their transformative potential.

Table of Content

Chapter 3

- How the Rabbit R1 Works With Your Apps
- Integration with Common Apps
- Advanced Features and Capabilities

Chapter 4

- Case Studies: The Rabbit R1 in Action
- Personal Use Scenarios
- Business and Productivity Applications

Chapter 5

- Navigating the Challenges
- Addressing Privacy and Security Concerns
- Troubleshooting Common Issues

Introduction

The Dawn of AI in Everyday Technology

In the realm of technology, the advent of Artificial Intelligence (AI) marks a watershed moment, revolutionizing how we connect with our world. AI, once an idea confined to the realms of science fiction and high-end research labs, has now seamlessly integrated into our daily lives. This integration signals a new era where intelligent machines not only help us in difficult tasks but also enhance our everyday experiences.

The proliferation of AI in everyday technology is not just about smart gadgets; it's a wider trend towards more intuitive, responsive, and personalized technology. From smartphones that understand our preferences to smart homes that adapt to our living habits, AI is changing the user experience. Its effect is apparent in various sectors, including healthcare, where AI assists in diagnosis and treatment plans, in transportation with the advent of autonomous vehicles, and in the realm of personal assistance, where AI-driven virtual assistants are becoming increasingly sophisticated.

This broad adoption of AI is a testament to its potential to make technology more accessible, efficient, and attuned to our needs. It's not just about the technology itself, but about how it allows us to live better, smarter lives.

Enter the Rabbit R1, a pioneering example of how AI can be harnessed to revolutionize our interaction with everyday apps. The Rabbit R1 is not just another gadget; it's an AI-powered assistant designed to easily integrate with and improve your app experience. It epitomizes the convergence of AI with everyday technology, giving a glimpse into a future where our interactions with technology are more fluid and intuitive.

The Rabbit R1 stands out with its advanced AI algorithms, capable of understanding and executing a wide range of app-related chores. Whether it's managing emails, making meetings, or even engaging in more complex activities like graphic design or data analysis, the Rabbit R1 is equipped to handle it with ease. Its sophisticated AI engine is meant to learn from your preferences, adapting over time to offer a more personalized experience.

Furthermore, the Rabbit R1 promotes user-friendly design. It is not meant only for tech-savvy individuals but for anyone who seeks to streamline their digital interaction. With its intuitive interface and easy setup, the Rabbit R1 demystifies AI, making it accessible and beneficial to a wider audience.

In this book, we will delve deeper into the capabilities of the Rabbit R1, studying how it can transform your interaction with technology. From its core features to real-world applications, the Rabbit R1 serves as a beacon of the AI-driven future, a future where technology not only serves our wants but anticipates them.

Chapter 1

The Rabbit R1: An Overview

Design and Features

The Rabbit R1 stands as a paradigm of modern technological design, blending aesthetics with usefulness in a way that appeals to both tech enthusiasts and everyday users. Its sleek, compact form factor is crafted to easily integrate into any personal or business space, symbolizing a blend of sophistication and user-centric design.

Key features of the Rabbit R1 include:

1. Advanced Touch Interface:
The Rabbit R1 boasts a high-resolution, responsive touch screen, offering an intuitive interface that simplifies movement and control.

2. Voice Command Capability:
Equipped with state-of-the-art voice recognition technology, the R1 allows users to connect through voice commands, making it more accessible and hands-free.

3. Customizable User Experience:
Users can modify their R1 experience through customizable settings, such as

app preferences, notification management, and display themes.

4. Seamless App Integration:
The R1 is meant to work with a wide array of applications, ranging from productivity tools and social media sites to advanced creative software.

5. High-Speed Connectivity:
With built-in Wi-Fi and Bluetooth capabilities, the R1 ensures fast and reliable connections to different devices and online services.

6. Portable and Durable:
Despite its sophisticated technology, the R1 is built for durability and portability,

allowing users to depend on it both in static and mobile settings.

Understanding the AI Technology Behind R1

At the heart of the Rabbit R1 lies its advanced AI technology, a mix of machine learning algorithms, natural language processing (NLP), and predictive analytics. This AI framework allows the R1 to not only perform tasks but also to learn and adapt to the user's habits and preferences over time.

1. Machine Learning Algorithms:
These help the R1 to analyze user interactions and improve its performance,

ensuring a more personalized and efficient experience with each use.

2. Natural Language Processing (NLP):
This feature allows the R1 to understand and respond to voice commands in a natural, human-like way. It's not just about recognizing words but getting the context and intent behind them.

3. Predictive Analytics:
The R1 uses predictive analytics to anticipate user wants. For example, it might suggest sending a follow-up email after a meeting or remind you of upcoming chores based on your calendar.

4. Data Security and Privacy:

Recognizing the importance of data security, the R1 includes robust encryption and privacy safeguards to protect user information.

5. Continuous Updates and Improvements:

The Rabbit R1 is built to evolve. Regular software updates not only fix bugs but also bring new features and capabilities, ensuring that the R1 stays at the forefront of AI technology.

The Rabbit R1 represents a major leap in AI-driven personal technology. Its blend of sophisticated design, user-friendly features, and cutting-edge AI technology positions it as a vital tool for anyone looking to improve their digital experience

Chapter 2

Setting Up Your Rabbit R1

Installation Process

Setting up your Rabbit R1 is meant to be a straightforward and user-friendly process, allowing you to start experiencing its benefits with minimal hassle. Here's a step-by-step guide to getting your R1 up and running:

1. Unboxing and Initial Setup:

Carefully unbox your Rabbit R1, ensuring all components, including the power adapter and setup guide, are present.

Place the R1 on a stable, flat surface near a power source and where it can easily connect to your Wi-Fi network.

2. Powering On:

Connect the Rabbit R1 to the power source and switch it on. The device will begin a boot-up sequence, indicated by a welcome screen on its display.

3. Connecting to Wi-Fi:

Follow the on-screen steps to connect the R1 to your Wi-Fi network. This step is important for enabling online features and updates.

4. Software Update:

Upon first connection, the R1 may ask you to download the latest software updates. It's important to finish these updates to ensure optimal speed and security.

5. Account Setup:

Create a user account straight on the R1 or via its companion app (if available). This account will be used to change settings and preferences.

6. Device Pairing:

If you plan to use the R1 in conjunction with other smart devices or your smartphone, follow the instructions to pair these devices through Bluetooth or Wi-Fi.

Initial Configuration and Customization

Once your Rabbit R1 is installed and connected, the next step is to configure and customize it to fit your preferences and needs:

1. App Integration:
Access the main menu to pick and install your preferred apps. The R1's interface makes it easy to view and add apps from a curated list.

2. Voice Recognition Setup:

Train the R1 to know your voice for hands-free operation. This may involve repeating a few phrases so the gadget can learn your speech patterns.

3. Customizing Settings:

Personalize options such as monitor brightness, sound volume, notification preferences, and more. Tailoring these settings will improve your user experience.

4. Scheduling and Automation:

Use the R1's AI capabilities to set up schedules for routine jobs or automate certain activities, like sending out daily emails or organizing files.

5. Security and Privacy Settings:

Ensure you review and change the security settings, including setting up passwords or biometric authentication, to protect your personal data.

6. User Guide and Help:

Familiarize yourself with the user guide and help section offered on the R1. This resource can be useful for troubleshooting and learning advanced features.

By following these steps, your Rabbit R1 will be fully set up, personalized, and ready to enhance your digital interactions through its innovative AI powers.

Chapter 3

How the Rabbit R1 Works With Your Apps

Integration with Common Apps

The Rabbit R1 is meant to seamlessly integrate with a wide range of widely used applications, enhancing their functionality and your interaction with them. This integration spans various categories, from work and communication apps to entertainment and creative software.

1. Productivity Apps:

The R1 syncs with apps like calendars, email clients, and task planners. It can plan appointments, sort emails, and set reminders, optimizing your workflow and saving time.

2. Social Media Platforms:

For social media apps, the R1 can handle posts, track notifications, and even analyze trends, allowing you to stay connected and informed without being overwhelmed by the volume of content.

3. Entertainment and Streaming:

When integrated with streaming services, the R1 can suggest material based on your viewing history, control playback, and manage subscriptions.

4. Smart Home Controllers:
The R1 pairs with smart home devices, allowing you to control lighting, temperature, security systems, and more, all through a unified interface.

5. Health and Fitness Apps:
For health-focused users, the R1 can track fitness goals, watch health stats, and even suggest workout routines or diet plans.

6. Financial and Shopping Apps:

The device can assist in budget tracking, bill payments, and online shopping by managing accounts, tracking expenses, and looking for deals.

Advanced Features and Capabilities

Beyond simple app integration, the Rabbit R1 offers a range of advanced features and capabilities that leverage its AI technology:

1. Learning and Adaptation:

The R1's machine learning algorithms allow it to adapt to your usage patterns and preferences, making app interactions more personalized and efficient over time.

2. Predictive Functionality:
Utilizing predictive analytics, the R1 can anticipate your wants. For instance, it might suggest sending a follow-up email after a meeting or remind you to buy a gift for an upcoming birthday based on your schedule and past behavior.

3. Voice and Gesture Control:
Advanced voice recognition and gesture control features allow for hands-free operation, making it easier to use apps while multitasking.

4. Multi-App Coordination:

The R1 can coordinate between different apps for complex jobs. For example, it can cross-reference your schedule and weather apps to suggest the best time for an outdoor meeting.

5. Automated Content Creation:

For creative apps, the R1 can help in content creation, from drafting initial ideas to suggesting edits, using its AI-powered tools.

6. Data Security and Encryption:

The device ensures high levels of data security, employing encryption and other protective measures to safeguard your private information across all apps.

7. Remote Access and Control:

Through its companion app or web interface, you can easily access and control the R1, managing your apps even when you're away from the device.

In essence, the Rabbit R1 works as a central hub for your digital life, enhancing your interaction with apps through AI-driven customization, efficiency, and advanced functionality. Its capabilities make it not just a gadget but a thorough assistant for a wide range of your digital needs.

Chapter 4

Case Studies: The Rabbit R1 in Action

Personal Use Scenarios

1. **Home Management:**

   - Case Study: Emily, a mother of two, uses the Rabbit R1 to streamline household chores. The R1 manages her smart home devices, controls lighting and temperature, and even aids in setting up entertainment for family movie nights. It tells her of family members' birthdays and anniversaries, and helps with shopping lists based on past purchases.

2. **Health and Fitness:**
   - Case Study: David, a fitness enthusiast, depends on the R1 for his daily health routine. The device tracks his workouts, offers meal plans based on his fitness goals, and monitors his sleep patterns, giving insights for improvement. It also syncs with his health apps to keep track of his progress.

3. **Learning and Hobby Enhancement:**
   - Case Study: Sarah, a lifelong student, uses the R1 to aid in her language learning and gardening hobbies. The R1 suggests daily

language exercises and tracks her progress, while also providing tips and reminders for plant care, depending on the season and her location.

4. **Personal Finance Management:**

- Case Study: Alex uses the R1 to handle his personal finances. The device tracks his spending, helps budget his expenses, and even alerts him about unusual account actions. It combines with his banking apps for seamless financial oversight.

Business and Productivity Applications

1. Small Business Operations:
   - Case Study: Lisa, a small business owner, uses the Rabbit R1 to manage her business activities. The R1 aids in scheduling appointments, managing customer questions via email, and keeping track of inventory through integration with her business apps.

2. Project Management:
   - Case Study: A project manager, Raj, uses the R1 to coordinate project tasks. The device integrates with project management software, updates job statuses, sends

reminders to team members, and even prepares progress reports for stakeholders.

3. Corporate Communication:

- Case Study: An IT company uses the R1 to streamline its internal communications. The device schedules meetings, sends out agenda and minutes, and handles the team's shared calendar, ensuring efficient coordination among employees.

5. Data Analysis and Reporting:

- Case Study: Nina, a data analyst, uses the R1 to help in data compilation and preliminary analysis. The device gathers data from various sources, performs initial sorting and analysis, and prepares reports, allowing her to focus on more complex analytical jobs.

These case studies show the versatile applications of the Rabbit R1 in both personal and professional spheres. By automating routine tasks, providing personalized insights, and enhancing efficiency, the R1 proves to be an invaluable tool in various scenarios, showcasing the practical benefits of AI in daily life.

Chapter 5

Navigating the Challenges

Addressing Privacy and Security Concerns

In an era where digital privacy and security are crucial, the Rabbit R1 addresses these concerns through several robust measures:

1. Data Encryption:

The R1 uses advanced encryption protocols to protect user data both in transit and at rest. This ensures that personal information, from app data to voice orders, is securely encoded.

2. Regular Security Updates:

To safeguard against evolving cyber threats, the Rabbit R1 gets monthly security updates. These updates patch vulnerabilities and improve the device's defense mechanisms.

3. User Authentication:

The device features multiple user authentication choices, including passwords, PINs, and biometric verification, to prevent unauthorized access.

4. Data Privacy Controls:

Users have full control over their data. The R1 allows users to set preferences for data sharing and storage, including options to delete data or restrict its use for certain apps.

5. Network Security:

The R1 is designed to operate securely within different network environments. It includes features like firewall protection and secure Wi-Fi connections to avoid unauthorized network access.

Troubleshooting Common Issues

Despite its advanced technology, users may face issues with the Rabbit R1. Here are some usual problems and their solutions:

1. Connectivity Issues:

If the R1 sees trouble connecting to Wi-Fi or Bluetooth devices, restarting the router or the R1 itself often resolves the issue. Checking for interference from other gadgets can also be helpful.

2. Software Glitches:

In case of software malfunctions, resetting the device to its original settings or updating to the latest software version can remedy many problems.

3. Voice Recognition Errors:

If the R1 struggles with voice commands, recalibrating the voice recognition settings and ensuring a quiet area during setup can improve accuracy.

4. App Integration Challenges:

For issues related to specific apps, checking for app updates or reinstalling the app can often fix compatibility issues.

5. Battery or Power Problems:

If the R1 experiences power problems, ensuring the power adapter is properly connected and checking for any damage to the power supply can be a quick fix.

6. User Interface (UI) Confusion:

For users finding the UI complex, consulting the user manual or online tutorials given by the manufacturer can offer clarity and direction.

In every case, Rabbit R1's customer support plays a crucial part in assisting users. They offer detailed troubleshooting guides, customer service hotlines, and online help for more complicated issues. This comprehensive support system ensures that users can navigate and resolve any challenges they face while using the R1.

Chapter 6

Comparative Analysis

Rabbit R1 vs. Other AI Gadgets

To understand the place of Rabbit R1 in the landscape of AI gadgets, it's crucial to compare it with its peers. This comparison focuses on key areas like functionality, user interface, AI capabilities, and overall user happiness.

1. Functionality:
The Rabbit R1 excels in multifunctionality, effortlessly integrating with a wide range of apps and smart devices. Other AI gadgets often focus in

specific areas, such as home automation or fitness tracking, but may lack the R1's broad applicability.

2. User Interface (UI):

The R1's intuitive and user-friendly design stands out. While many AI gadgets offer sophisticated features, they can sometimes fall short in offering an accessible and easy-to-navigate UI. The R1's touch and voice command features set a high standard for user experience.

3. AI Capabilities:

The Rabbit R1's advanced machine learning techniques and natural language processing are on par with the best in the market. Its ability to learn and adapt to individual user tastes gives it an edge over many competitors, which may offer more static AI experiences.

4. Design and Portability:

In terms of design, the R1 is known for its sleek, modern aesthetic and portability. While other gadgets also boast impressive designs, the R1's focus on a balance between form and function is particularly noteworthy.

5. Price Point:

The R1 is positioned in the mid to high-range market group. Some AI gadgets are more budget-friendly but offer fewer features, whereas others are more expensive but do not greatly outperform the R1 in functionality.

Market Trends and Consumer Feedback

1. Increasing Demand for AI Integration:

Market trends show a growing demand for AI integration in everyday gadgets, an area where the Rabbit R1 is well-positioned. Consumers seek devices that not only simplify chores but also provide personalized experiences, a strength of the R1.

2. Consumer Feedback on R1:

Users generally praise the Rabbit R1 for its ease of use, versatility, and the efficiency it brings to handling digital tasks. The ability to control various parts of their digital life from a single platform is highly valued.

3. Critiques and Areas for Improvement:

Some feedback points to areas for improvement, such as the desire for even wider app compatibility and improved battery life for more extended mobile use.

4. Competitive Edge:

In comparison to its competitors, the R1 is often praised for its balance of advanced features and user-friendly design. It's seen as a gadget that's not just technologically advanced but also truly useful and accessible.

In summary, the Rabbit R1 holds a significant place in the AI gadget market. Its strengths in versatility, user interface, and AI capabilities align well with current market trends and consumer preferences, although there's always room for enhancements in response to user feedback and changing technological advances.

Chapter 7

The Future of AI Gadgets

Emerging Trends in AI Technology

The landscape of AI technology is rapidly changing, paving the way for innovative trends that are set to redefine the future of AI gadgets:

1. Greater Personalization:

Future AI gadgets will likely offer even more personalized experiences, using advanced algorithms to better understand and predict individual user tastes and behaviors.

2. Increased Interconnectivity:

The concept of the Internet of Things (IoT) will spread, leading to a more interconnected network of AI gadgets. This will enable seamless communication and coordination between different devices, enhancing customer convenience.

3. Enhanced Natural Language Processing:

Improvements in NLP will help AI gadgets to understand and respond to human language more correctly and naturally, making interactions more intuitive and human-like.

4. Advancements in Machine Learning:

Machine learning capabilities will continue to advance, allowing AI gadgets to learn and adapt at an unprecedented rate, improving their efficiency and usefulness over time.

5. Ethical AI and Privacy:

As AI becomes more integrated into daily life, there will be a stronger focus on ethical AI development and enhanced privacy protections to meet growing concerns about data security and moral considerations.

6. AI in Healthcare and Accessibility:

AI gadgets will play a more prominent role in healthcare, offering personalized health tracking and assistance. Additionally, there will be a focus on making AI technology more available to individuals with disabilities, enhancing inclusivity.

Predictions for Future Developments

Given these emerging trends, we can predict several developments in the world of AI gadgets:

1. **Autonomous Functionality:**

AI gadgets will become more autonomous, capable of performing complex tasks with minimal human involvement. This could range from self-organizing calendars to autonomous home management.

2. **AI-Driven Predictive Maintenance:**
Gadgets will be able to predict and plan their own maintenance, reducing downtimes and prolonging their lifespan.

3. **Emotion Recognition and Response:**
Future AI gadgets might have the ability to recognize human emotions and respond correctly, enhancing user interaction and support.

4. **Integration with Augmented and Virtual Reality:**
The convergence of AI with AR and VR technologies could lead to more immersive and interactive experiences,

changing entertainment, education, and professional training.

5. Eco-Friendly AI Solutions:

As sustainability becomes a global concern, AI gadgets will likely be designed with eco-friendly materials and energy-efficient technologies.

6. Advancements in Quantum Computing:

The integration of quantum computing with AI gadgets could significantly enhance their processing capabilities, allowing them to handle extraordinarily complex tasks.

In summary, the future of AI gadgets is set to be not only technologically advanced but also more personalized, interconnected, and ethically aware. This progression will surely open new horizons for how we interact with technology and its role in enhancing our daily lives

Chapter 8

User Guide and Best Practices

Tips for Optimal Use

To reap the benefits of the Rabbit R1, here are some best practices and tips for its optimal use:

1. Personalize Your Settings:

Spend time customizing the settings to fit your preferences. This includes setting up your favourite apps, adjusting notification preferences, and personalizing the interface.

2. Regular Voice Training:

Periodically retrain the voice recognition feature to improve its accuracy, especially if you notice any difficulties in command detection.

3. Utilize Scheduling Features:

Leverage the R1's scheduling capabilities for chores and reminders. This can help streamline your daily routines and improve productivity.

4. Explore All Features:

Familiarize yourself with all the features and functions of the R1. Often, users don't utilize the device to its full potential simply because they are unaware of all its possibilities.

5. Integrate Multiple Apps:

Maximize the R1's productivity by integrating it with a variety of apps. This centralized control can greatly streamline your digital interactions.

6. Use Security Features:

Take advantage of the R1's security features, such as data protection and user authentication, to protect your personal information.

Maintaining and Updating Your R1

Proper maintenance and regular updates are crucial for ensuring that your Rabbit R1 continues to work effectively:

1. **Regular Software Updates:**

Keep the R1's software up to date. Regular updates not only bring new features but also contain important security patches and performance improvements.

2. **Clean and Care for the Device:**

Physically clean the device regularly, ensuring that the screen and sensors are free from dust and dirt which could impede performance.

3. Monitor Battery Health:

If your R1 is a portable model, check its battery health. Regular charging and avoiding extreme temperatures can help increase battery life.

4. Check Connectivity:

Regularly check your Wi-Fi and Bluetooth connections to ensure the R1 keeps a stable connection with your network and other devices.

5. Backup Your Data:

Regularly backup any important data saved on the R1 to avoid loss in case of technical issues.

6. Seek Professional Support When Needed:

If you encounter any complex issues or malfunctions, call the manufacturer's support team for professional assistance.

By following these guidelines for optimal use and upkeep, you can ensure that your Rabbit R1 continues to be a reliable and effective assistant in your day-to-day life.

Conclusion

Summarizing the Impact of Rabbit R1

The Rabbit R1 stands as a testament to the amazing advancements in the field of artificial intelligence and its integration into daily life. This AI-powered device has redefined the way we interact with our digital world, giving a seamless, intuitive, and efficient experience. The R1's ability to adapt to individual user preferences, its versatility in handling a myriad of tasks across different apps, and its user-friendly interface set it apart in the burgeoning market of AI gadgets.

From managing household chores and personal health routines to streamlining business operations and enhancing productivity, the R1's wide array of functionalities demonstrate its significant impact. Its role in automating mundane tasks, providing personalized suggestions, and improving decision-making processes exemplifies the practical benefits of AI in everyday life.

Final Thoughts on the Role of AI in Daily Life

The emergence of devices like the Rabbit R1 signals a broader shift in our connection with technology. AI is no longer a distant, complex idea; it has become an integral part of our daily lives, reshaping how we work, connect, and entertain ourselves. The R1 exemplifies how AI can be harnessed to not just augment human capabilities but also to give a more personalized, efficient, and engaging experience.

Looking forward, the role of AI in daily life is poised to grow even more important. With advancements in machine learning, natural language processing, and predictive analytics, AI will continue to become more sophisticated, intuitive, and essential. The Rabbit R1 is just the beginning of this trip. It paves the way for a future where AI is smoothly woven into the fabric of our daily existence, enhancing our lives in ways we are only beginning to imagine.

In conclusion, the Rabbit R1 is more than just a gadget; it's a glimpse into a future where AI allows us to live more productive, connected, and fulfilling lives. As we embrace this future, the potential for AI to revolutionize every part of our existence is both immense and inspiring.

Appendices

Technical Specifications

1. Device Dimensions:
   - Size: [Specify measurements in inches or centimeters]
   - Weight: [Specify weight in pounds or kilograms]

2. Display:

   - Type: [LCD, LED, etc.]
   - Size: [Specify screen size in inches]
   - Resolution: [Specify in pixels]

3. Processor and Memory:
   - CPU: [Specify chip type and speed]
   - RAM: [Specify size in GB]
   - Internal Storage: [Specify amount in GB or TB]

4. Connectivity:
   - Wi-Fi: [Specify standards, e.g., 802.11 b/g/n/ac]
   - Bluetooth: [Specify version]
   - Ports: [List possible ports, e.g., USB, HDMI]

5. Operating System:
   - [Specify OS and version]

6. Battery:

- Type: [e.g., Li-ion]
- Capacity: [Specify in mAh]
- Estimated Life: [Specify in hours]

7. Audio and Microphone:

- Speakers: [Yes/No, and give details if any]
- Microphone: [Yes/No, and give details if any]

8. Voice Recognition:

- Technology: [Specify technology and traits]

9. AI Features:

- Machine Learning Algorithms: [Describe quickly]
- Natural Language Processing Capabilities: [Describe briefly]

10. Security Features:

- Data Encryption: [Specify type]
- User Authentication: [Describe means, e.g., password, biometric]

Frequently Asked Questions

How does Rabbit R1 learn and change to my preferences?

The R1 uses machine learning algorithms to analyze your usage habits and preferences, allowing it to tailor its responses and suggestions over time.

Can the R1 control other smart home devices?

Yes, the R1 can integrate with and handle compatible smart home devices such as lights, thermostats, and security systems.

Is my personal info safe with the Rabbit R1?

The R1 uses advanced encryption and user authentication methods to ensure your data remains secure and private.

What types of apps can the R1 connect with?

The R1 is compatible with a wide range of apps, including productivity tools, social media, streaming services, and more.

How do I change the software on my Rabbit R1?

Software updates are usually automatic. You can also directly check for updates through the device's settings menu.

Can I use voice control with the R1?

Yes, the R1 features advanced voice recognition technology, allowing you to perform chores and control the device using voice commands.

What should I do if I face technical issues with my R1?

Consult the user instructions for troubleshooting tips. If issues persist, call Rabbit R1 customer support for assistance.

Is the Rabbit R1 portable?

Yes, the R1 is intended for both portability and durability, making it suitable for a variety of settings.

How do I ensure my R1 stays up-to-date?

Regularly connect your R1 to Wi-Fi to receive and install the latest software updates and feature improvements.

Can I use the R1 for business purposes?

Absolutely. The R1 is versatile and can be used for a range of work applications, including scheduling, email management, and data analysis.